HOTHOUSE

HOTHOUSE
Tracy Ryan

PUBLICATIONS
2006

Published by Arc Publications
Nanholme Mill, Shaw Wood Road
Todmorden OL14 6DA, UK

Copyright © Tracy Ryan 2006
Design by Tony Ward
Printed and bound by CPI Antony Rowe,
Eastbourne, East Sussex, UK

ISBN-13: 978 1904614 13 5
ISBN-10: 1 904614 13 2

ACKNOWLEDGEMENTS
This book was first published by
Fremantle Arts Centre Press in 2002.

Some of these poems originally appeared in
*Atlanta Review, Canberra Times, Island, Jacket, Lines of Sight,
The Nightwatchgirl of the Moon* (ed. Ian Duhig),
Poetry Review, Prism and *Verse,* and some were broadcast
on Radio 5UV Adelaide, Australia.

The quote on p. 69 is from Richard Tipping's 'Mangoes'
in Les A. Murray, ed. *The New Oxford Book of Australian Verse*
(Melbourne: OUP, 1986, p. 353).

Cover illustration: 'Souvenir no. 2'
by Robert Demachy
[gum bichromate print c. 1901]

The Publishers acknowledge financial
assistance from ACE Yorkshire

International Editor: John Kinsella

To John

Contents

Half

pomegranate, half
gone, your
cut face wincing
with exposure

still you maintain
your composure, a mere
contraction the sole sign
of loss

your gloss
was always internal
the double
removal of core, of
kernel in infinite
dispersal, you

split as you will
with heat or some
intrinsic logic
I can't dissect.

Compact and self-
satisfied, replete
with myth and real
history

spilt over my childhood
gate in a far country
taken for granted
gone to seed
bleeding your cordial

but forgotten
until the arrival
of this parcel
lobbed from the south
of France
meant for my daughter

your ruby mouthful
red potential
old bombshell

Extremities

Jack whom my husband as a child
in a hot land
met flaming at the door and saw
at once *the fear of God*

warned of by Dad
when I was young
on account of your eye for
whatever's proffered: toe poking
uncovered from the bed

I know your tread,
greedy Hades,
deadhead.
I dreamt you as the distant must.

You came
to visit, left cards,
letters Nana had
from the trenches: *the coldest cold*
that ever colded.
Lifelong, I've neared
your kingdom.

Now you come into your own,
the thrill's worn thin.
Each little chill a kick

under the table
shutting me up
as intimates will.

Or pull at my vein, a reminder
who holds the string;
turning that toe to permafrost,
small earnest.

Hothouse

If things could be forced like this
feelings produced
                    out of place
sticky plumbago a blue
mild as your eyes, or the wild
throaty red of hibiscus
slapping at me, an arranged
memory –
not what I'd choose.
                    Home
I never thought to miss.
Specimen too, I sweat
under glass, space false
as a moonbase or slow
deserted zoo. What you
may visit but never know.

Mallee Root

Not what we understood
as wood, this warped
and twisted thing
that had lain hidden,
dry truffle, under a surface
we knew only from
Lost in Space, the jaundiced
wastes stippled with sheep-
skulls plundered by city teachers
for our 'contour drawing',
distortions
rendered functional
as their ligneous kin
here on The Farm –
smug lump presented like
a fact they had on us,
the country cousins,
when we lost at *Squatter*
instead of *Monopoly*,
fixed on the grey brain with folds
unravelling,
Medusa self-petrified,
slow burning.

Meat

For me it wasn't a trivial thing, even though people
tell me, "Worse things happened in the war.' It is not
easy to go back...
  – Hans Kupperfahrenberg, on the ham he stole
  from a French farmhouse as a German soldier in
  1944, and replaced with another in 1999

All of a piece and curiously like my own.
What's a little death between friends?

They'd get us if we didn't get them first.
It was after I saw my abdomen all stitched up.

The very sight of it made me retch.
Sorry, but I was only a boy and there was

No other choice but to fight. We go over
And over the same ground which would

Swallow us up if we didn't take measures.
I saw myself with this head bobbing all separate

Like a puppet, or rejected god. Deflated.
Eat what's put in front of you. Something

To cut your teeth on, oral sadist. What you carry,
The elision the wreck is founded on,

The murder we all have in common.

15

On-line

Fell into this
because it was offered

came with the territory:
a mask that stuck

shoes that took
and went on dancing

and like everything else
it came with a hidden charge –

my past pitching up again
and again from the dark

pool of the screen
beamed in like *Star Trek*

as disembodied bits
I know only

from the nerves they hit
and miss, no hand

to recognise
but a canny truthfulness

that identifies
in spite of the uniform font.

How they scout and trawl
for me, the ones

I tried to shake off
or simply let drop,

how we persist
in ourselves, apparently

whatever name
we assume, and the blind faith –

At last
I've found you, she writes,

though that site could already
be years old, dead star

winking out –
and should I want

to evade, I could pretend
her words never arrived

left to hang
like that message

from a friend who died
hours later

that I could not
delete.

The Bower

for Kathleen Stewart

Stiff fingers of grass and twigs
propping up nothing
she's ever seen, this nest is
a shrine to absence
she nonetheless surrounds
with bits that might appeal,
accepting the limits set, in every
conceivable nuance of blue.
Sharp signals into the void
or offerings to a god she
wouldn't know was there
except that something
takes up her gestures,
leaves out and rearranges –
almost a message returned.

The Peacocks

Passe-partout

Useless as beauty to ponder
why he should choose
this particular window
to set off
his passive artistry

though choice is too
much agency, he
is a random happening
sudden to himself
as a triggered erection

entering this frame
more as part-
montage than mise-en-scène.
Most often gone
before you sense
anything.

But this morning
into this evening, that spread
of tail rigid with quivering, quills
vibrant at base like a vast
particoloured cunt at
high pitch, all jewelled want and no
resolution.

Passion

Queen or femme
hammy as a silent
black and white
sprung at once
into colour, the eloquence
all squall in the talkies.
Not his element.
Indolent thing, he's made
for a stage that won't
take him. Plays it cool
with a fan like that?
Who is he fooling, strolling
between engagements.
If he didn't exist
we'd have to invent him.

Peahen / Paean

Her skirts her hair
seem always plural
a fluid movement

I had abjured
but like a spectre
unreal as water

that we are made of
she ripples through me
nothing is salvaged

sandbag & dredger
against a drenching
O my own

medicine,
come in and
lose me again –

these were gods'
secrets, I thirst
at her mirage

straining at clusters
I never tasted.

Polymorph

Finely perverse
        in your resistance
to placement,
        thing or being

sky-formed surely yet
      earth-indued
weighed down with
      fantastic garland

in the tragic tail
      you rise again –
Medusa-head or
      maenad.

March

London grime still
        under my nails and in my
                nostrils. We cut a swathe where
they once used to cut such
                a swell. The City they say that
        does nothing productive, only *facilitates*
flow from poor to rich. We held back
        the traffic. Park Lane
                the parting of the Red Sea. Where
        is the far shore? Our words would be
only drops in a fouled ocean. World
        and fouled a consonantal rhyme.
                An off-rhyme? Our words
        reduced themselves, rhythmic,
fell into step. Stressed feet. The faces
        hung at railings as gazing into a stream.
                Some will take home a sliver,
        a splinter, a pang of conscience.
Others simply annoyed at not being
        able to cross. We wandered through
                each shuttered street. This is the poem
        with no ego-I. This is the way we wash
                our hands. The Manichaeans
                were considered heretical
                because they saw evil
                as an equal
                and opposing force to good,
                where it was supposed
                to be a corruption of,

       or digression therefrom.
Grace infused
     or attributed. Depraved
or deprived. Who will answer
     from the angel hierarchies?
        If we
     cry out No No
     No. If we should die before we
            wake.

'Cambridge considered as the Cocos & Keeling Islands'

The whiskey on your breath
Could make a small boy dizzy;
But I hung on like death:
Such waltzing was not easy.
   – Roethke, 'My Papa's Waltz'

Where you found your perfect Scandinavian
        fivestar dreamroom, only the bed
        was inches short, and hard as the bed of a monk –
no place was a place to get straight in –
        and the mini-bar had to be smuggled in
        to ease your retreat, and the hosts themselves
teetotal, if this was your tropical
        island you were stuck with me like a blank
        book, where you wanted talk
and got my silence, dumbfounded I
        took your pain regardless,
        packed as a squash ball in a closed space.
Trace, you said, but the sentences
        never went where you intended, they
        rebounded, and I was
a little girl again, watching the red
        Celtic lines of my father's
        harried brow and neck, I am not big enough
to handle this, if I stay
        long enough, mute witness, perhaps
        it will pass. Mid-tears
you laughed and apologised, asked
        if I knew that Hopkins wrote those hymns
        we both grew up on.

Dublin

Home that is not my home
love that is asymptote
birthmother I don't own
matter and template

furnishing ghost and bone
impossible place
city of sun
through smoky glass

what may be known
approximate
reflection
of Gorgon's head

touch of a glove
no caress
where I believe
like Thomas

weren't we all
beneath the church
beneath her heel
God-out-of-reach

loveletter
again and again
to deliver
without return

Dalkey

Because a friend lived there once
and timing is always awry –

and the train sides
with the small sea

that might as well
be everything

sea that meets and parts
in every gesture –

the one constant.
The road down

crowded with villas
hoarding the outlook

we see through chinks –
another life

till the coast opens
and the island beckons

too perfect and close
to be borne

all that we wanted
boat after boat with no one

to row us out.

Avowal

The mountains are framed
in my window,
a theatrical set. I imagine,
imagine my ashes scattered there
a truce, a placating
where I've never been
where a mother's people
kept a father's down
broadly speaking,
so setting a pattern
he might call on for
justification
as he began
to believe his own publicity –
maudlin and drunken. Tinahely,
County Wicklow, so hidden
so open, and even now
spelt wrongly, odd as that slip
of the tongue that insisted
her side was from Scotland.
Originally.
I invoke each fact
to push back the dank cloud
of cowardice, child
calling names: Tinahely,
Waterford, Dublin, Henry,
Bridgett, Stephen, Francis, us.

Kin

What a legacy:
to have the face
of Ned Kelly
known to most
behind a stark
helmet or mask
or in the case
of the famous painting
not even there.

How many would know
that young photo?
the Ned of before
or after the self-grown
armour
with its one
uncovered spot

our point of entry,
the myth like so much
crustacean accretion,
an exoskeleton

the life within
vivid and free
of cynicism,
completely human

carry this
ambiguous kinship
as you can, Stephen,

embody
what we would plaster over
with words,
impasto, blunt strokes
that fumble at living.

Closure

We shake our heads and rue
first leaf litter as if
it had never been before
and the story was new

but where you come from
it's dark always and there
you will return soon, late,
whatever I plot or

ascribe; I'm what you wrote,
once, as a kid when you tried
out the other hand
and found a wobbly likeness,

an opposite, but one
you couldn't count on,
the line, the season, untrue
and yet your own.

Cycle

Still leans on
the same spot
    where you left
it by moonlight
    for the new
owner
    mute and
obtuse   cast-off
    metallic chrysalis
so close
    for a season
unmarked
    as I am
servant of
    purpose
no sign
    of transfiguration
but of slow
    decline
by rust I
    never noticed
when you were
    with us.

Yellow Roses

Seated, on edge
we bracket them

undead and drinking
surrogate sugars

colour eked out
beyond their due

sustained like false
hopes

'disordered vision'
of jaundice.

I slice the stems
to draw it out

they barely wince
as I compose

this rearrangement
each rose emptied

of content
and reinvented.

I tell you
jealousy

but play no part in
their actual statement

they hold the floor
their other life

irrelevant,
something we have to

work around,
jealousy

not meant:
yellow alert.

Holy Island

Accessible only
sometimes and perilous
the rest
this place I piece
together
little nuance
to my mental map
of England
now I know space
by what's between us
opponents at chess
where there's no
mate but endless
reconnaissance,
small difference
across the road, in transit
or at the very limit –
absent in any case.

Castle Hill

Two weeks and the grass
has withered under our feet

Nothing will regenerate
the particular moment

The ghost of movement
your camera cannot fix

Words that ripple
unanswered

Images the wind wants
to tear from tentative fingers

Easily marred, afraid
to grasp as I should.

Exchange

I warn you about *foreigner*, how
it can only be used for yourself;
those soft distinctions not conveyed
in textbooks. You say, aside,
isn't it odd how people always remind
us of other people
as words do with other words, and never
settle in one place. I watch you daily
do battle with untold demons,
terrain so known to me I can't
foresee the pitfalls. But I'm learning
contours of your language from the points
you halt at in mine. And intonation
distant as music strained
through someone else's Walkman.
I'm picking up phrases like pebbles,
shingles, broken slate, piecing my way
to a sense of the shore.

Two Views

In beads

The rings of age that will never reach her
settle already around
her neck. Iconic begets *beautiful*
more sixties than herself. His choice. Beads
strung out and hanging as the hours
she made them in, yoke, circle
draping the breast at first unnoticed. Regally
swaddled, a marble baby. Stare me down.
Overpower the gaze in.
Ring, bauble, sequin, nipple,
single eye.

In beads only

Always one step further than asked for
and yet she kept them. Fronted
like a brace of medals. He protested:
a visible line from the just-shed
clothing. Hands fan without discretion
what's hers alone to keep or
give away. Forget the costume.
Bead and flesh are fused,
breast identified: there is no Janis
but this.

Chandler Sonnet

There's a limit to what you can get away with
Calling ironic. Unless you mean that iron the
Pansy just doesn't have in those damn bones but heck,
He's easily disposed of, like the paper
Left over from any stencil, the stockpile
Of images that render presence, make you what you are:
No big blonde in black suede refusing
To give back light or that other bubble only
On two legs for when you want her there.
But legs her sister surpasses. Supine
For your delectation. We failed all of us
At being quite so stupid but our every word
Gets heard in the same speech balloon anyways.
What you are is something. Altogether more solid.

Two after Rodin

1 that way inclined

deux femmes enlacées
two women intertwined or
        interwoven
swaddled in Virgin blue they can't
        maintain

wrestling   bearing down
turmoil in the coiled hair
        dual Medusa
interlocking torsoes   faces lost
monozygotic   pale
pupal stage in the growth of
a many-limbed goddess

cannot emerge from
background flat as grey stone
air of graffiti
                or cave painting

three-legged monster
perched on nothing
or is it lying down

could be aerial view or
up on pedestal

how coldly furiously sketched in

this moment of meltdown
too wet to be sculpted

what resists his
third-dimensional
intervention

hommage à ma grande amie Judith Cladel

(some of my best friends etc)

2 *eternelle idole*

and the mistress the one
eternally young
accepts the homage
being only half as bound

he kneels encumbered
mouth blind arms back as if
bobbing for apples
it's that self-conscious

her pose is the mermaid
tongueless but legged now
accepting her due   accepting
things will remain out of kilter

just so
with one plaster hand she guides him
the other
    she draws away

Cranach's *Venus*

No need to ask how she comes
to be balanced there, barely behind
her veil that's more red rag than
modesty, only the colour's
dropped out, a skein of wind
that hints: *to enter in these bonds,*
is to be free, desire to flee
the course of this life, tear out
of this nightmare and into the body's
morning again, her flesh, that double
puppy-fat chin, those hardly
ready breasts and feet still spatulate
fantasy forest encroaching upon
the split and distant city, to have it back
as it was, recurrent idol, yes, but
only eternal as their reproach: don't
change, don't grow, don't show
any suggestion of who
you are

Hyacinths

O you may wear your rue
with a difference
   – Ophelia

You should have known
but there must be a first time
you don't see coming

turn on your heel
as if for a last
and futile glimpse
of your attacker

as if identification
could fix them
making you less
susceptible

but you are hooked now
these pastel barbs
deceptively soft
on a first encounter

dipped in the stuff
of swoons, Laertes' sword

you will come back
to black earth and
incredulity

how such beauty
could have been

forever
you will be waiting
for their return

Hydrangeas

1

Nodding-off cluster of heads
or gaudy cheerleaders
depending on mood

you were the blue register
of a layer
we couldn't uncover

the outward visible sign
of an inward
disposition

under my brother's window
as if you knew
he'd die young and we'd strew

that pit with just such blue.

2

Our argument
the old one

between aesthetics   \
and science

you were explainable
par excellence
with binary
tendencies

we liked to gender.
Pink at my window.

Fight with me now
we'll get nowhere

two opposites true
at once.

3

Eventually I'll come over
to your side

it looks different
from ground level

remember the earthworms
we'd sometimes turn

out and hastily rebury
too aware now of

another order.
The hours we spent lying

in dirt and counting
each blade of grass
as if they meant it.
The hard blood of the eucalypt

the wattle's sticky wound
our own innards

lurching up.

4

Named for the cups
that cloud and mass out

to render their opposite:
concave and convex

like the lenses
of his science kit

like the simple cells
that form the complex

that is my body
that will simplify

again, like his, the petals shed
colourless and drifting.

Liebchen

You women all die at fifteen
– Diderot

I never was your
   dear little thing
nagging, niggling
   shadow right through
your brilliant career:
   you were Judy D.
and Debbie Harry
   in one, and outraged when
I said so, you were
   there on the day
we started Year One, me glum
   and dark as a pudding
you in your chopped straw
   bowl-cut, six summers of
strands green at the end
   from too much
swimming
   skinned knees and
Brownies
   right through to high school
diminished and neutered
   I worshipped you –
Liebchen,
   you called me, with sarcasm,
or only
   my surname

you were lead in the musical
   you were the girl
a future film star fell for
   and you spurned him
inner thighs bald from a life
   on horseback
breasts fine and light as
   new pears
you were one of those girls
   from the right
side of town, and when we went
   to the costume dance
you let me go with you
   cowgirl and Indian
odd couple that wasn't
   when I beat you at French
your only second
   you swore I cheated
when you kissed Bob Green
   from the school play
I was humiliated
   on your behalf
though he did
   use the word 'impart'
correctly
   and that impressed me
you belong to a lost list
   of girls who disappeared
that is to say

who never needed me
except for killing time
    making up numbers
or having an audience
    a way to rehearse
the real thing, like blowing
    on milk bottles
before the flute lesson
    and because of this
you have entered me
    more sharply
than the keenest note
    you have not
grown up, you have lodged
    there and work your magical
infection through every
    vein, dear little thing
Liebchen.

In the absence of hair

Je la veux agiter dans l'air comme un mouchoir
– Baudelaire, 'La Chevelure'

it was the other differences we saw
all those markers we'd learned in school
and never proved/ your tongue behind
my flattened teeth, or in the crevice of
my alien ear (it tasted bitter, like yours)
together we tested hypotheses of the body
can you kiss Caucasian
or is it elsewhere
this elusive presence – no *langoureuse Asie*
I was a sea of white Australian faces
in the shop where they wouldn't serve you
I could be flat as the posters
on bus stops that shouted
get out
you affected the silks and the sandalwood
the Chinese vodka clear as candour,
deaf to no desire but
making yourself heard –
shaved your head and wore
your good butch beauty
like a placard I could never
quite read and why should I
expect to, there was nothing
for me to run my fingers through
there was no Political Issue
for me to tease out

as I might have wished to
there was only the sweet real nothing like
this and resistant you

Clinical

Indignity of death wanting
to enter this way
here, of all places, where they flowed
with essence of goodness

but where would you choose, exactly
to let him in?

Clamped, flattened and scanned
from every angle
resistant, like fuzzy barcodes or
bad blueprints

guided by pain alone, the bumps
that ache like milk
no longer needed
but are something different

skewered and sampled and then restored
to personhood
each woman leaves dejected or
elated, nothing between them.

An ink ring, indelible
where he made it a thing
so it wouldn't feel wrong to do this.

A little gauze cross, like a botched
suture, to mark the spot.

'Joseph's Coat'

Dubious gift
like the one it was named for
the houseplant
a foreign concept,
something I've never kept
with my knack for killing off
by half-deliberate
neglect, as if
only so much flourish
can be faced –

my ideal
the bare wall or floor, austere
and essential, no chink
where tendril
might creep in, plain
as a Dutch picture my
interior, small room
for green.

And yet this eruption
of colour
I now must find
a corner for, acceding to
needs which are after all
minimal –

a bloom not even
floral or open but in the vein,
muted and pure, content
in its spiritual
element, water and light
and that
indirect.

A Preservation

for my father

In his absence the figs dripped
and the ants feasted.

I came each day and watered
as I should

renaming each comer
of the marred garden

this is how
it might have been.

He wouldn't eat them
so the three trees

fruited and festered
as if he enjoyed

somehow the waste
aspect

the running to seed.
So I climbed and stuffed

my face with them
but for the odd one pierced

and numb with ants
like Bunuel's hand

and what was left over
I claimed for jam

weeks and weeks of it
like congealed time

so many yields
condensed and bottled.

Wasp Diary

God bless the corners of this house
And be the lintel blest
And bless the roof-tree overhead
And bless each place of rest...

1

The first day we realise
this is serious
I read her Dennis's poem
and leam
the frost will get them.
But the frost doesn't come.

Summer's extended
just for the wasps,
underwriting their expansion.
They are dependent on it.
Their technology too has limits.

A movement nearly electronic,
fridge and computer
unnerving me now
with their connivance,
turning to wasp song.

A whole wall of them
within the wall
and arching out now

into the roof-tree,
a human house
gone live and porous.

What have we done
to deserve this?

2

When the rains come
the mould on the inside surface
maps the spread of their
would-be empire,
powdery black
instead of pink.

At first we think it
innocent,
but with the wasps
it all makes sense
the way extraneous symptoms
fall together
at the knell of a word like cancer.

A relative menace –
en masse, they might kill us
as long as we stay passive

which is by choice and not
by nature.
                    Yet in reverse
they haven't a chance.
The repertoire of slaughter
is all on our side.

Okay, so we'll retreat.

    3

Her room is the first
we seal off, she is
holed up there
out of love –

her world shrinks further.
We have become voices
behind the door.
I will not let them get her.

We bring her food.
We escort her places,

take her out despite
the newly cruel
October weather,

the wasps by now
grown bold on success
drunk on a false
interior summer.

4

In comes the hit man
to do our dirty work.

Warm and gentle
he respects his target.

Six feet, he says, like the depth
a dead man sinks to

or the length of a man on his belly –
creeping sniper,

nest with a mission
like the cyst I harboured

so big the doctor wondered
how it could fit there
without something bursting.

A surgeon, then.
A bedside manner.

Four times he visits
and it still isn't over.

He's sorry, but we should go now
and wait for the all-clear.

5

The flat they have given us
in the interim
mimics the contours
of the other

with subtle distinctions
so we trip over ourselves
the door that opens outward
the switch that isn't there.

And on the ground floor
so we know
the noise we must have been making,
thinking ourselves insular
when cellular,
stirring things up there.

The furniture
ours in another shade,
as if this were a dream-world

or that set of off-colour images
we call memory.

Like the wasps shifting strategy
testing another point
of entry, we move on beside ourselves,
biding time till we can return
to the scene of the crime.

6

They should have fled
the moment their nest was thwarted.

Instead, they turned inward
certain they weren't mistaken.

They could have gone anywhere
or is there a kind of conditioning,

internal directive we simply
can't read?

7

Our flat has that fake look
of purity after trauma.

The polite reception
for a brother's funeral.

The repainting
after an axe murder.

How do you live there?
The chairs, though, left up

on the tables, our normal clutter
gone straight now, like an addict

after a near miss.

Green

It began with marigolds
that never showed
alongside the bungalow
when I was twelve

I learned you could tend
and tend without
recompense – you either
had it or not.

Perhaps it was earlier –
those broad beans we all
cajoled on damp cotton-
wool in primary school,

soil-less, dislocated
as an idea without
context, one blunt end
marked with a sly smile

or was it a lid? the blind eye
of a coconut where
they told us the milk
came out, though it looked shut

like the secret aperture
our baby sister
must have come by
that I tried to picture

somewhere near
the upper thigh
thinking it must seal over
when out of use.

I was clueless
as the broad beans, isolate,
generic, never given
a real chance

feeding no one.
Each lonely monad
aligned on the sill
worshipped in term-time

as if that would boost them,
then on the holidays
forgotten and gone
to mould.

Against the grain

Poppy-heart, the short span
of a passion

uprooted, that shoots again –
weeds are a matter

of definition, but there's also
self-identification:

arable just a label.
I take my name

from association
contingent being

cornflower or cockle
insinuating

through fields of need
am shepherd's needle

text or terrain shot through
with longing

flagrant, I queer
the beige pitch of wheat

bad egg
black sheep

live fly in the unctuous –
I persist

however disturbed
the ground

to hold
my own.

She gives

mangoes are what parents & parliaments
warn against
  – Richard Tipping

Thick-skinned in an English winter
greenhorn but ripe
enough this time to section
and apportion

blameless perhaps
visceral as flesh and
bone though I'm
no carnivore

and find myself helpless –
such an embarrassment
of riches, roundly
voluptuous, I must

control this gift you bring
with poem and knife
and anecdote
reduce the fruit

hypostasise
the feeling –
too much to manage alone
too gross for metaphor

the mango is merely there
bluntly luscious
already more
than eaten.

She takes away

Pink as anything
that will not open

except by chinks
and then surrender

not an inch,
the tulips you left me

slouching now
their potential moment over

their meaning anyone's guess –
scentless perfection

like saintliness
ever expert

to seduce us
and leave us hanging

barely flushed and unexcitable
delicate, a nest of fledglings

whose gape is quaint
and hunger measureless

but capacity not great
chaste as a slip of silk and just

as torturous
in the making.

Piano

Small walls and the furniture
too large, as in a dolls' house
or a Dutch interior
the swollen disproportions
of a dream;

a baby grand and you playing
Bach and Satie
as my grandmother played the Polonaises
and my mother the 'Moonlight' Sonata

suddenly the hunger
to pick it up again, dropped stitch,
to let fingers go as they know because
it was trained into me
every morning

or because I was bom to it
and let it go, wasted and taken for granted
like water; this our idiom
I've abstained from
out of some foolish notion

of imperfection, forgetting the pure pleasure
the insidious mastery of song
that makes the child's heart beat faster
as I stand there
wordless but listening
with my arms around her
in the chill spring.

Outside the glasshouse

I lose you for a moment and then catch sight:
crouched under twin camellias you approach
with the lens as one might
a timid animal,
allowing them soul.

I hold back: double pink, double red,
such richness best at a distance
or I am swamped
unless it's instinct
tells me not to intrude

between you and the beauty
of your own response.
Starvation for months
and now this glut of colour
almost insulting in its abundance.

Not all at once
but bud by snub bud they unloose
their vivacity, raised cups
we'd slake our hurts at
if we could only trust

they'd last – *longevity*
and faithfulness, the book says
so you store an image
to paint them from
like tracing and retracing
a lover's name.

Iris Poems

Single

He said: if you strip them back they will
yield again and again.
Blue profusion in my dream – while the child
grew and complicated in me, the iris-
rod blossomed, flossed, unstoppable
in my grasp.
Men friends were knowing, Freudian – women
stared and insisted I must name her Iris.

I called her
what I intended, I meant to
play, pay the story out long and confident
as a kite string from my fingertips,
ignorant of the wind's
inexorable mouth, iris-innocent then.

Quickening

Fund of food or pure energy, this ugly
stump – how we misjudge!
When do we call it life?
The whole thing hidden there
in a simple corm. I was struck dumb.
Suddenly we were
everyone's property, she and I – they'd prod
and comment, say how

we'd be better off, I should be hard,
a termination.
No one could love the cold garden,
the bare earth I worked in then.

Stealth

Rhizomic, we know
no real separation –
like your gift of two stems
from the armful a woman
gave you in turn –
a lateral movement,
propagation
of understanding.

Untrammelled, they crowd
and must be divided,
heavy feeders.

In town they are regular
you wouldn't know
their nature –
the distance aesthetic
passion erotically stunted.
Somehow they recognise
each other.

I have no longer
any time or room for them
mother only now,
though they still catch me
springing out where
I never planted
queering the path after thaw

or sending a near relation
jonquil or freesia
to ruffle the surfaces.

Found / nomenclature

*'Don't starve your irises
or make them compete.'*
– American Iris Society.

Trim the velvet
ruby eruption
behind closed doors

comet trails
distant nebula

dusky challenger
lady friend

epicentre.

My little Persephone

comes and goes
like these irises

mother a long
confinement

my howling loss
blights the exteriors

I am half winter
and she is half Hades'

somewhere we meet
and continue
as though nothing had parted us.

Landing

When I enter you it is always
with the feeling of having forgotten something;
a taint of betrayal not even the
disinfectant spray can disguise, a sense
not that the years or the foreignness
could be stripped away, but that
there really is nothing underneath,
that the offending matter
(wood, straw, fur, seeds, alien soil
ingrained in my skin) moves with me,
with us, the blood
on certain hands, and that your notion
of being some kind of virgin, O most continent
of continents, should have been
lifted long ago from your shoulders, and
though I know these precautions are necessary and
would never willingly transgress, I understand
them too as metaphor: if we're any lady at all, then,
Lady Macbeth.

Homecoming

As if the hothouse contents had
got loose and gone reeling,
as if a cast were
peeled off and the limb long since
had forgotten the discipline of muscle.
A profusion of blue, the sky, the plumbago
unruly as I remember it, and the blooms
a riot on bougainvillea.
As if my insides had unravelled
and willed themselves
to words: the ancients thought
our gut the seat of emotion. Heart
too clean and purposeful
an emblem for this sprawl, this
letting it all find space. A release,
a return to the wilderness.

Moreton Bay Figs

... of all places of condemnation ...
  – convict song

1

In the small park, parrots flash
and riddle the black canopy
with colour from the upper world,
raining spent fruit, decay
by trickle-down effect.
Below is dank, fermented –
almost comfort
against such clarity
and rolling with figs underfoot
where each great root
set like a trap
reminds me to watch
my step.

2

In the large park, three gaps arch
between trees whose green has melded
into solidarity, barricade
past which a light pools, familial.
If I could blend in there
and never emerge – if I could
brace myself like that!

Limbs that taunt with
impossible horizontals, a stasis
equal to any onslaught.
We shall not be moved.

3

Walking the road
to Leederville
my way is lined with them,
learning to tread
so I accommodate
their gravelly underside
with a marred but feasible
gait, I cleave to their shade
being of and not
of these parts.

4

The parrots are at it again –
too quick for the camera
or I might send you
a glimpse of heaven, bereft,
rent and put back again.
How deftly they sever and get

to the gist of things, the unpicking
how systematic.
But the tree's skin
is thick and the heart unshaken.

Regeneration

for John

In this implosive heat you open
me as we used to peel
hibiscus

but it wasn't you then, it was
other children –
I am remembering

you back into
the start of me
because you are dusted

everywhere like
pollen
or volatile powder

right to the core
this reaction
obliterates thinking.

I am the pink and glistening
white folds we filleted and wanted
to eat though we knew

from the mute perfume
this would do us no good
so we left them

splayed and abandoned
all over the garden, our bliss
in destruction and sureness

of coming again.

The Last Orchid

Core of the bunch, propped limp
in a vase now too big
where the rest fell away
pretty quickly – the mundane
carnation, the prim
trimmed edge of the chrysanthemum.
When you brought them I knew
the past was in there
somewhere, like leaven for
dough, a starter culture –
cut but not yet spent, they couldn't
be all bland, just needed my discernment
my word to bring out their bloom.
What has happened to us?
We relax and thicken
into our ease, our containment,
let others do the talking,
amble like cattle in daisies,
Weena awaiting the dark
underground – and there are always
flowers, cut flowers
to accompany our every passage
like those gifts the Egyptians placed
with their dead, we are bled into things
till quite white and used, but I
refuse to give up the fight, I will
address you now as the girl you were
and ignore the orchid

mere symbol unable to inspire, a woman
is not a flower, though her flesh
be as grass and her spirit wilted.

Oleander

An old truism, that beauty
can be poison
though to be frank
I never found it
so lovely: petals always
a little rank, bruised and
has-been, something
used up before the
world began.

And the knife-like leaves I
teach you now to watch for
pretending this is
defence for you and the
smaller children
when really I want you just
to see it, bright wilter,
oily presence I've detested
a lifetime; just to say yes, Mum, I
recognise it.

Fragile Cycles

for David E. Musselwhite

Fourfold, the white spider orchid
    repeats at the gateway
    to the cemetery

where we didn't expect it
    coming here nineteen
    years now

where no one can really trespass
    and the purple Curse
    and the red-green flare of pain

of kangaroo paw
    are even domestic
    to this season – surely

we have seen everything
    there is to see here
    our big lives were over

when we laid him down
    and proved each bloom
    transitory thereafter

predictable
    as each shed cell
    called it a cycle –

yet these small, sparse
    tentative gestures
    too new and artless for

flags of truce
    take their place here
    at the entrance

become now our point
    of departure.

Cowslip Orchids

for David E. Musselwhite

1

Imbalance
    as if the artist
    left unfinished

fretted capillaries
lopsided
    blood in a splayed
    open yolk

seen up close
precision emblem
    metallic   faux-unique

picking out
thick verticals of sheoak
    so dark!

Lit wick
    redeeming the mass

too fine for that
ascendant eye
    scanning expanse
    for furry pulse

snagged on our gross
intrusive movement
    human shield
    or density

that might proceed
    oblivious

conversely

that a small orchid
might enter
and set off
    like detonation

transfigured   alone.

    2

En masse, a via lactea
    inverted

fallen starlight
    soured and yellow

this earth no mother
    too porous
    for gender.

Salt at the heart
 as we expected

which is no heart
 but a sure absence

the tang of it
 on lips

even before
 we speak.

You might think
 they led somewhere

but they are random
 clusters

clones   a proliferation
 gilt and centreless
 as any lode.

You must feel your way here.

3

Which of us is gone
which away from

this is a third space
word-made   uninhabited

the flowers are asterisks
contested passages

if flags   then yellow alert

nothing less certain
than what the world gives

a waxen solidity
     that passes

grass that receives
our tread and erases
all flesh is

     yet how we grasp.

Metaphysical

If I think for a minute of the globe
between us, it becomes
too much, it inflates
to absolutes and ultimatums,
thinking us mere sublunaries, dull
mortals – but our souls, one soul
surely, are never more
than a silken hair's breadth
out of kilter. If we must
be down-to-earth, then only
as the hemispheres themselves are,
dissimilar yet matching exactly
torrid and bright
where the edges, imagined, meet.

Australia

I'm looking at you with the squint
of distance and rapprochement, the way
we reappraise an ex
    how did I ever
    what was I thinking
and the tired old affection that
never quite fails us

you in your Anzac Day 'best', and I notice
you even manage a land-rights flag
up there among the
    rain-flogged and flapping
    bunting, though I know
underneath the sensitive-new-age act
you're still at it

with that woman the loo-walls call
'Sweaty Betty', your bit on the side
and the Yankee nuclear
    floozies (a boot in every
    port) not to mention domestic tyrannies,
will you ever grow up? but
no, you nations are all the same

whatever the name or rhetoric –
boys will be boys and the men
they're knocked into must have
      their mid-life crises
      some of us never did fit
the Bill Bloggs Joe Blow she'll be right
scenario, we were hoping for something

different, trying to stand on our own
      thirty-six million or so feet.

Biographical note

TRACY RYAN was born in Western Australia but has also lived in England and in the USA. She has worked in libraries, bookselling, editing and community journalism, and has taught at various universities. She is especially interested in foreign languages and translation. She has two children.

JOHN KINSELLA (Australia)
America – A Poem
Lightning Tree
The Silo: A Pastoral Symphony
The Undertow: New & Selected Poems
Landbridge: An Anthology of
Contemporary Australian Poetry
ED. JOHN KINSELLA

ANTHONY LAWRENCE (Australia)
Strategies for Confronting Fear

THOMAS LUX (USA)
The Street of Clocks

J. D. McCLATCHY (USA)
Division of Spoils

MARY JO SALTER (USA)
A Kiss in Space

ANDREW SANT (Australia)
The Unmapped Page

ELIZABETH SMITHER (New Zealand)
A Question of Gravity

C.K. STEAD (New Zealand)
Straw into Gold
The Right Thing
Dog

ANDREW TAYLOR (Australia)
The Stone Threshold

JOHN TRANTER (Australia)
The Floor of Heaven

10
Writers
Writing

Lochwinnoch Writers

Writers
Writing

Lochwinnoch Writers

Grimalkin Press

2006

Grimalkin Press
19 Currie Place, Cooper's Wynd
Glasgow G20 9EQ

ISBN: 0-9553786-1-3, 978-0-9553786-1-4

The publisher acknowledges the financial
assistance of the National Lottery Awards for All.

Typeset and designed by Grimalkin Press.

Cover designed by Christine Brown.
Ten Writers Writing Logo designed by Ginny Davies.

Printed by: printing.com@tangerine
49 Cowane Street, Stirling FK8 1JW
Email: stirling@printing.com / Web: www.printing.com

Contents

Introduction

Gerry Stewart, Tutor

I started working with the Lochwinnoch Writers in 2004 through the Workers' Educational Association and the Renfrewshire Council. Running for about a year, the group felt they needed a tutor to offer lessons on different aspects of technique and style. Though the members were at different levels of experience, they had agreed that they wanted to be taught more about the writer's craft, not to just share their own work every week.

Teaching the group is a challenge, while they are serious about their writing, there is an informal social atmosphere that keeps us on our toes mentally. No session is ever boring. They have varied interests from rhyming poetry, to children's stories and science fiction so we cover a range of subjects to ensure everyone finds something helpful including lessons on basic grammar revision to the intricacies of the Japanese haiku style of poem and how to get published.

My goal is to challenge their opinions on what they believe is good writing and help them to learn from different styles and genres, to understand the choices the author makes when creating his work. If the students don't like a certain writer's method, they can express their preferences with this knowledge. As a result I believe this has benefited their own writing. They make informed decisions about how they are going to craft and present their work and this is apparent in the pieces we have included in this collection.

Our WEA funding finished in 2005 and Susan Stewart of the Renfrewshire Council recommended we apply for further funding to run the group. She put us in touch with Carin Coyle of Renfrewshire Volunteer Services to obtain grant money from the National Lottery's Awards for All Scheme. Part of the funds was set aside to keep the classes going, but some of it was to produce this collection of poems and stories as a showcase for their talents and a chance to increase awareness for the group in the local community.

Ten writers, from different backgrounds and experiences brought together under one cover, each offering their own dishes to the feast. The stories and poems travel from Lochwinnoch to Orkney to Africa, covering styles from haiku to humorous fiction and an historical essay. We hope you enjoy this small sample and find something to whet your creative appetites.

Acknowledgements

The Lochwinnoch Writers would like to thank the staff of Workers' Educational Association, Renfrewshire Council, East Renfrewshire Volunteer Services, National Lottery's Awards for All Scheme, the McKillop Institute and Lochwinnoch Library. With special mention to the WEA's Karen Cosh and Jackie Howie, Susan Stewart, Karin Coyle and to Head Librarian Margaret Sweeney for allowing us to use the Lochwinnoch Library out of hours and to Janet Stirrat for making sure we're well looked after during our classes.

Thanks to Christine Brown of Crafts of Calder Gallery and Framing for the amazing cover illustration and to Ginny Davies for coming up with the title and logo design.

Joyce Allwright

Descriptions

Long auburn hair swinging as she walks. Black boots making a sharp tattoo on the pavement. Red coat with black fur collar turned up, very trendy.

"She's got my boots on," said my 8 year old grand daughter, "and they are not clean like mine, Granny."

Oh dear, one indignant look from the long haired one. "She's got a dragon tattooed on her neck, it looks fierce, doesn't it, Granny?"

I can't help but notice the vivid blues and greens and reds which almost encircle her neck. I do not think this tattoo suits her, but it would be a sorry state of affairs if we all followed the same beat of the drum.

Now the long haired girl speaks, her accent throws me. I can understand the villagers and can just about understand the Glasgow talk, but this is like a foreign language.

My grand daughter comes to my aid. "Don't you shout at my granny," says a stroppy 8 year old, "Else I will use my Jujitsu on you."

This angry out-burst makes the girl laugh and the incident is forgotten. When this auburn-haired creature laughs she is quite pretty. I bet the boys like her smile and green eyes.

Suddenly the bus appears and off she runs to catch it .

"Granny, can we go to the tea shop now? I'm hungry."

We enter the tea shop and there she stands making up her mind for creamy hot chocolate with flake and her favourite pink icing on a long finger bun.

"What are you having, Granny, digestives and tea? When you are very old I'll give you your injection." All this said with a dazzling smile.

Oh, the joys of being a granny.

Haiku

The chrysanthemums cannot bloom
Until the rose dies.

Sea crashes on the shore
Retreats
Beach is swept clean

Rain falls
Earth is replenished
Flowers grow

The Will

"Well, I'm having the silver tea pot. I don't care what anyone says," said Aunt Maud.

We were all of us crammed into the limousine which took us from the crematorium to the solicitors' office.

Not being a blood relative but only related by marriage to my sweetheart of a husband, I held my tongue and kept my thoughts to myself.

What a family! There they all sat like vultures waiting to get their share of their brother's will.

Aunt Maud with her silver tea pot (she hopes), Frederick, Sidney and Bernard all anticipating something.

"I don't see why you are here, Henry?" said Frederick, "You're only his godson."

"We were asked to come," I replied.

Frederick shot me a menacing glance but said not another word. Just gave a supercilious sniff and looked out of the car window.

Feeling pressure on my hand, I looked at my husband who mouthed silently, "Let it go".

"We're here," said Sidney (the creep) and we all went into the will reading.

The solicitor Mr. James Selby ushered us into his office and said, "Now, ladies and gentlemen, before I read the will, perhaps you would like to see this video your late brother made?" The family were not pleased but consented to watch the video.

"Well, hello there," said a voice on the TV screen, "If you think I've left any of my estate to you perishers, you can all take a running jump. You miserable greedy lot.

The only people here that have shown me kindness and thought are Queenie and Henry, so my dears I leave you, Henry, my books and you, Queenie, the pearls. Wear them and think of me occasionally, won't you dear?

My sister and brothers won't get a penny out of my estate, and don't try and contest the will because I have seen three Harley Street specialists who have declared me sane and in full charge of my faculties. You rotten lot, I have left my estate in a trust fund for the disabled and poorly-off students. It's to be called the Leefield Trust. So there."

Then their deceased brother blew the biggest raspberry I have ever seen.

The screen went dead and then pandemonium broke out. Maud had hysterics, the brothers used the most appalling language, worse than dock workers use. Even porters at Smithfield Meat Market could have taken lessons from the brothers. While this commotion continued office staff rushed in and tried to sort things out.

"Ladies and gentlemen, please, the will is in perfect order. You may all have a copy of it."

"You know what you can do with your copy, don't you?" snarled Sidney.

"How come you," he pointed towards me, "Get the pearls?"

"Well, they wouldn't go well around your neck, would they?" I replied, and then the brothers decided to start on Henry.

That's when they made a very bad mistake, Henry turned into a fighting tiger. For such a mild man he proceeded to castigate them very severely. I have never known a man to say so many nasty things without swearing, I suppose being a lecturer in English and Drama helps.

With Henry's outburst the sister and brothers exited, vowing retribution but Mr. Selby said they had not got a leg to stand on, or words to that effect.

On saying goodbye to Mr. Selby and thanking him for all his help, we left the office – me with my pearls and Henry with the key to his godfather's house and library.

"I still don't know why he left me the pearls?"

"He left them to you, Queenie my love, because of all the little kindnesses you did for him over the years."

"You as well as me," I said.

"True, but what clenched the trust he left was because you couldn't afford to take up your scholarship when you were young. It's a good thing you didn't because otherwise I would not have met my clever mature student and married her.

So come along, darling Queenie, let's drink to my godfather's memory and celebrate his life."

So we did and, being rather wicked, we toasted his sister and brothers. It never pays to anticipate what you can inherit at a will reading, but it made our champagne all the sweeter.

Clive Briggs

Computer of the Mind

I switch on,
Stagger into activity,
Blinking, twitching, painting pictures,
Bewitched, no work achieved, playing
Flying aimlessly to the next screen,
The next cult phase
Mesmerised by poorly appreciated power.

Keys are pressed, wheels grind,
Disks inserted,
Activity awakes
Output appears,
Memories stored or lost
According to whim.
Somewhere deep inside.

An enclosed box from which peripherals peer,
Clever but temperamental,
Mind slowly decaying, losing relevance.
Outdated windmills powered by the breeze,
Whirling, twirling, driven by eerie eddies;
Trying to cope with modern ways.
Abilities recycled in modern form.

Ultimately the great switch off
Leaves a blank screen.
Memory erased,
No place to record
The great beyond.

Village Groups

Old oak smoky black beams,
Yellowed low ceiling
Bright blond busty barmaid,
Flightily flirting with tired tipplers.

Hum of mid-week gossip,
Chatter of flighty young mothers,
Secretive smiles of lost lovers
Drowning deep in each other eyes

I sit silently watching,
A facet of village life
Sipping a sour guest beer
Inferior to the pub's own brew

Beyond yon windowed wall
Brew beers of better taste
Each distinct, different in toxic content
Out with the door the village houses,
Families, similar but distinct

Why must the lonesome traveller
On life's tempestuous trail,
Be always looking for the new
And always doomed to fail?

To be at home secure,
Is what the traveller craves
But company is what he seeks
To set his spirit free.

Alpine Village

Villages sprayed on the mountainside,
Speckle marks on a harrier's egg.
Brooded over by towering peaks
Of an alpine massif.

Came the avalanche.
Sounds of distant thunder on the high top
White shroud over the peaceful valley floor
No footprints, no lights at day's end.

Spring returns, ground thaws,
Graves are dug
Villagers sleep in the earth
Watched by the brooding shrouded peak.

A solitary eagle circles
Determined to regain the familiar haunt
Warily watching the snow curtain
Painting white the mountain's mourning weeds.

Endeavour is not enough
To tame the mountain rage
One cannot subjugate
The mountain Gods to personal desire

Winter returns again.

A Natural Life

They told me in school that god was good.
I did not meet him in Physics or Maths
But tanned with tawse and cut with cane
I learnt.

To listen, to read, to think,
Reject mythical theses, unproven 'facts'
Shun theism.

It took thirty years to find my god.
In craggy and crumbling rock, reaching for the sky
Debris falling to the valley floor
As shattered scattered screes.

On green grass
Stock speckled meadow,
Spattered by fat mooing milk producing herd.

In sparser upland grass,
A paler green
Home to hefted sheep,
The soaring bird and sweeping wind.

Shelter, a solitary rock, rain lashed
More welcome than the broken byre
Bracken filled, dressed desecrated stone.

A turbulent stream stumbling down hill
To join a tumbling rushing crashing flow
Washing scoured rock.
Hastening down to a rolling sea

That carries all before.
Casts it on some lonely shore
Seaweed home for shrimp, crab and fly
In brown earth turned in winter's blast
By tractor-towed plough,
Seagulls clamouring for unearthed worms.
Land harrowed, seed scattered, bedded
                              in a rich brown field.

Late autumn springing bright green winter wheat,
Standing afresh, signifying the year to come,
Cyclic start of the season's yet to be.

I heard the prelate cry that God was love,
But when I listened I heard him not
In the clamour clash and clang of war.
He was not there.

In the thunder of bombs,
Dirge like aircrafts drone
Crack of rifle shot, well aimed
I found no comfort.

No rounded reassuring love
In the arms of war,
In bitter recrimination
Rant and ravings
Cleric or priest proclaimed.
Mars' heroic glory gone, abused

Prayers in lofty ecclesiastical buildings
Unanswered lay.

The choirs chant unheeded
The choreographed service
Just a magnificent production
In a dated theatre.

Played to a dull dozing dwindling congregation.
In the old cold uncaring cathedral church
Home to a weekend's fancy dress party

I returned to hill and natural world,
Found a peace,
Prayers answered
A cautious calm companionship.

Accepted
Accepting.
Partnership,
On the wheel of life.

February

Strange tortured twisted sky,
Clouds wind driven fragmented, racked with pain.
Sleet showers, snow and sun.
Snowmen standing gardened,
Like Russian dolls on Easter Island shore,
Will fledgling spring of saffron tinted flowers
                              survive the winter blast,
Dying gasp of the earth's Dark Lord.

Moira Bromley-Wiggins

Strawberries

Travelling on a red murram road in a cream clapped-out Beetle are an old 'muzungu' woman and her loyal servants. They are being pursued by rebels in a hijacked UN jeep.

Temporarily deluded, she believes the bag she is clutching is full of huge strawberries, but in reality it's sweet potatoes. They all know they can never out-run the rebels, who are whooping gleefully at the sport of the chase and waving their rifles in the air.

A group of people can be seen ahead. They are now her destination, in the hope of distributing the strawberries.

It becomes clearer as they get near, that this is no friendly assembly here. One set is distinguished with rifles, the other is clearly cowed by them.

As they get out of the Beetle and approach the group, the riflemen order the unarmed to sit down in line on the hillside. Even the shade from the trees is not on their side and the sun glares down on them. Then the UN jeep arrives, screeching unnecessarily to a swirling halt.

As an elder, the muzungu insists on distributing the strawberries amongst the captives, the group they have perceptively joined. The rebels sneer and smirk at her foolish misguided authority, but assent by turning to greet their newly arrived allies.

Her companions gasp and stare aghast at her audacity with hollow-eyed terror. But the mostly old men and women still gather round. She notices one younger woman holding a baby, shadowed by a child of about eight.

Untying the bag she has a moment of mad clarity and earnestly tells them to start an argument while she gives out the food as a distraction for the child to run into the bushes and hide. Unaccustomed, as fatalists, they stare incredulously at this notion to take some control of their situation.

Her associates quietly reiterate what she has just said. The mother desperately pleads for the baby to go, too.

'It's too risky,' urges one, 'The baby may cry and give away the boy.'

'Besides they'll notice the baby gone but might not the child,' adds another.

Wretchedly, she concedes.

The hissing conversation draws attention and they are called upon to line up. Believably their argument starts and escalates into a full blown row over the food. Some one has been given more than another. The boy, prompted with a shove, reluctantly runs into the bush.

Shots are fired into the air. A stout woman steps out from the rebels. She is wearing some kind of uniform, her fat legs bulging over the boots worn beneath her tight grey skirt. She must be their leader. She chastises the group for their futile argument. Do they not see they are going to die?

Too briefly they realise, for the first time in their lives, that the white foreigner with her aspiring play acting had made them forget what they had always known.

They were going to die.

The Dark

I jump awake, but the nightmare that startled me is instantly forgotten to the fear I find myself in. It's a black black darkness. I'm about to fall into an abyss of nothing. Before crying out, I'm conscious of the catch of my breath, so reason I can't be dead but, devastated, conclude that maybe, this is how it feels.

Cautiously I crane my neck to peer around the room. To try and discern any shape or chink of light in this macabre dark. I lift my hand, splay my fingers then bring it towards my face. It abruptly hits my nose. I've gone blind.

Searching for something tangible, I find the fine mesh of the mosquito net tucked tautly into this mean slatted bed. Through the thin mattress I feel 'its' shoulder blades, elbows and ankles reflectingly digging back into mine.

Cocooned in the net I'm not afraid of the micro-skittering

feet across the low headboard. Higher up I hear fast pattering followed by faint crunching. I wryly hope it's a hated cockroach being devoured by the jet-eyed gecko, rather than one of those poor jumping creatures with little control of all those legs contorted around him.

From the 'widip' croak and the few plops that follow I imagine the frog has left through the gap under the door. I'm anxious that he doesn't fall prey to the whirring bat or the audacious snake that settles with hissing sighs in my rattan ceiling. Amazed, I'm now consoled by the teaming wildlife that comes uninvited to my house (earlier it drove me to the sanctuary of my bed). It's the dung floor that attracts them. It has a surprisingly sweet odour, freshly smeared by the local women prior to my arrival at the mud hut.

Unexpected, there's a bamboo creak and a cough, my askari, the watchman must be stirring. Muted voices grow louder though still indiscernible, then fade as people pass my house probably to get water.

In a rush I tangle with the bedding, force a gap in the net, grope for my slippers then surge forward to the window catch and push open the shutters.

Immediately dowsed in brilliant sunlight. I smile relived at the bright bright Kenya morning.

Turning back to my bedroom all is clearly defined but I shiver with apprehension of the dreaded black night to come again.

The Dancin'

My Davy loves the dancin'
It's Ceilidh that's his niche
His face is all a beamin' doing
A St Bernard's or Schottische

So at Christmas and New Year
We go to keep his chin up
To Loch Lomond, tho' not near,
A Hotel called 'The Winnoch'

Joining tourists who flock there
For a festive Ceilidh treat
Thrilled to hear the music
As we all jump to our feet

They may be old and infirm
But it's not always the truth
Our aim is to include them
Remind them of their youth

My Davy loves the dancing
He's really quite a draw
It's great to see their faces
When he gets on the floor

The familiar Gay Gordons
The waltzes they all know
As the dances do get faster
They appreciate the show

He's a Dashing White Sergeant
Fairly kicking up his heels
His kilt swirling audacious
To all the jigs and reels

They gasp at the Eva Three Step
When he throws me in the air
They murmur with admiration
You'd think he was Fred Astaire

My Davy loves the dancing
He's more a Darren Gough
You know that cricket celebrity
Now he can't dance enough

Strictly Come Dancing's victor
Of both I'm quite a fan
He may not do the Ceilidh
but he dances like a man!

Soon we'll start the ballroom
In time, you never know
With practice and resolution
We may get on that show!

But really it's pure enjoyment
Meeting friends, keeping trim
And yes I love the dancin'
Especially with him.

James F. Carnduff

V.E.

"Grandpa, what did you do on V.E. [Victory in Europe] Day?"

"Celebrate, of course!"

"And how did you do that?"

"Let's start at the beginning, when War was declared."

"When was that?"

"Sunday the 3rd of September 1939. My father told us to be quiet and listen to the Radio as the Prime Minister Neville Chamberlain was to make an announcement at 11.15am.

My sister and I listened as the Prime Minister explained that the country was now at war with Germany as Adolph Hitler had marched into Poland and now occupied the country. Since we had signed a treaty with Poland, to support them in any war of occupation, we were obliged to go to war.

Being only 10 at the time it did not strike me the same way as it did my parents. My father was talking about conscription into the armed forces, possibly the Royal Navy as he had been an Engineer Fitter but now was in partnership with his brother in Architectural Ironmongery and Blind Roller Manufacturing.

Very soon after the Declaration of War all men under the

age of forty had to register with the Government for conscription. However, my father was fortunate that he had worked as an Engineer Fitter with Thomas White & Co. Ltd., an Engineering firm in Paisley. His expertise in making and fitting out Cartridge Gauging Machines made him important for the war effort. Therefore, it was back to Engineering he had to go. This was a change from his chosen occupation. Everyone had to make changes to their lifestyle.

On the domestic side, blackout procedures had to be adhered to."

"What are blackout procedures, Grandpa?"

"Instead of cream linen or cream paper blinds everyone had to have dark navy blue linen or paper blinds with side flaps to keep in the light. Maps could not be sold and the sign posts of towns, etc. were taken down.

At school we were all issued with gas masks which we had to carry with us at all times. I remember receiving my gas mask in a nice new cardboard box with a piece of string to go over my shoulder for carrying it. It was so well made that the box lasted about two days and had to be constantly repaired. Fortunately, later on, I managed to obtain a black tubular can which fitted my gas mask perfectly and my father attached a length of blind cord which allowed me to hang the can over my shoulder. Every week we had to practise Gas Mask Drill in the class. This took the form of wearing the gas mask and checking that you could inhale properly by being able to hold a piece of cardboard by suction to the mouthpiece of the mask. Quite a few people found the gas mask to be claustrophobic. I am glad that we never had to use them for real.

By January 1940, the Government imposed rationing and the use of points coupons became the norm. For example, sugar allowance was 8 ounces per person per week [about ¼ kilo]. Sweets and chocolate was 8 oz [about 2 medium size bars per month]. Eggs were in short supply but sometimes you were able to obtain a box of 12 dried eggs. The box was covered in grease-proof paper and came from America. This was a ration for 8 weeks for one adult.

I remember my mother making date jam and banana jam to eke out our meagre ration."

"Did you like the home-made jam?"

"Yes! It was better than nothing but was an acquired taste. However we managed fairly well because of the various vegetables we grew ourselves in our back garden. Everyone who could 'Dug for Victory' in their small gardens and allotments.

By 1942 white bread was replaced by a darker National Loaf which was healthy and nutritious. In June 1941 clothes rationing was introduced in a campaign called 'Make Do & Mend' and everyone made do with hand me downs.

My Scout Troop helped the War effort."

"In what way?"

"We collected waste paper in the form of newspapers, magazines and comics. One of the perks was to hunt through the bundles of waste paper for comics and spend time reading them.

A number of Senior Scouts, Patrol Leaders and Scout Leaders volunteered as message riders to cycle between Command Posts, Fire Stations and Air Raid Precautions Posts delivering messages etc. Unfortunately during a heavy raid in the Paisley area, when a land mine dropped on a First Aid Post one of our Scouts, John Farrow, was killed. This certainly brought the War much closer to our Scout Group. We still have a photograph of him in our Scout Hall. [The Bield]

It was round about this time that the Scouts were told that they would have to find new premises to hold their meetings. Happily for us we managed to purchase a large hut which had been partially damaged by fire. It had belonged to the Church of Scotland and was now no longer needed. Thus we eventually flitted lock, stock and barrel but it took a great amount of clearing, etc. to make it reasonably habitable."

"Did the War seem to last a long time?"

"Yes, it did, although I did not realise it at the time. It was just a way of life and you did not think of it in that way. I'm sure my parents felt it was a long time. When the Prime Minister, Winston Churchill, on Monday the 7th May 1945 made the announcement on the Radio that the War was over and that Tuesday 8th May was to be a national holiday to be named V.E. Day. We all breathed a sigh of relief."

"And what did you do to celebrate?"

"A good question! When people heard the announcement on the 7th May that the War was over they immediately downed tools and left the factories, etc. to celebrate. All the schools were given two days holidays on the 8th and 9th May. It is interesting that the local paper [Paisley Daily Express] did not print their newspaper on the 9th May but resumed printing on the 10th May."

"What was Paisley like during the 7th and 8th May?"

"There was a euphoric atmosphere. Everyone you met was smiling and very cheerful.

The Paisley Municipal buildings were flood lit and festooned with fairy lights. The War Memorial was illuminated by flood lights and all public buildings were draped in flags.

Side streets had buntings stretched across them. Paisley County Square and High Street were crowded with people singing and dancing. You could hardly move through Paisley Cross for the crowds."

"But, Grandpa, what did you do to celebrate?"

"Ah, personally, the jungle telegraph from the Scouts had sent round the school that anyone who could should meet [not in uniform] at 7.30 pm at the Bield!"

"Did you go to the Bield?"

"Yes! As a matter of fact, I arrived at about 7pm and was surprised to see a Huge Bonfire being prepared by the locals on the waste ground near our Scout Hut.

By 7.30pm about 12 of us decided to see what the centre of Paisley was up to, so off we ventured. We noticed, as we walked through the town that at every piece of waste ground bonfires were being lit!"

"And what were they burning?"

"Anything and everything they could find. I noticed that many of the Anderson Shelter bunks were being heaped on to the fires. Some were lit while others were in preparation.

Everywhere we went people were hanging out flags and bunting. Nowhere were the blackout procedures adhered to. I have never seen people so happy, kind and crying all at the same time; it was quite a unique experience.

We carried on out through the Cross passed the Kelburne Cinema and Paisley Ice Rink to arrive at Barshaw Public Park where crowds of people were singing and trying to dance to bagpipes.

There were a few slightly inebriated revellers paddling in

the boating pond. A few of us were competing to see who could jump over the smaller bonfires without getting singed.

We decided we had walked far enough and about turned back the way we had come. By this time it was beginning to get dark but with all the bonfires and the houses showing light, it was no longer a blackout night. In some places that had tarmacadam, bonfires had been lit on the streets. The tar had been set on fire giving a glorious light and smell.

We eventually stopped at a small café near the Paisley Library and each of us had a small bowl of hot mushy peas with salt and pepper to bring out the flavour. This was quite a luxury during the time of rationing.

Having fed the inner man we sauntered off back to the Bield just in time to see some of the local natives prying off planks from the Scout Hut. We chased them off. Our motto was 'No retaliation to provocation by natives!'

But to reinforce this we got buckets of water and drenched the outside walls of the Hut to discourage anyone trying to use the Hut as bonfire material.

As Scouts do, we had a mug of N.M.C. [National Milk Cocoa] and blethered until after midnight when we eventually wound our way home.

What a night! A night to remember!"

Geoff Cooper

In Paul Valery's "Cimetiere Marin", Sete, Languedoc

It is not your plasma noon
But under April sky at last
Tombs, trees and tenements incandesce

Far beneath, the harbour is a bright stone bow
Flexed for Africa, and the sea of odysseys
Lifts the fishing boats again towards the sun

Across vast horizons the great chameleon
Blue, gold, viridian,
Shines a million brilliant mornings once again

And a child, among the tombs,
– knowing everything — lifts her hands,
Jumps towards the sun,
Her laughter
Equal to the light.

But I arrive too early and too late
Walking the negative spaces of these tombs
Shadowing cross and pediment and chiselled words,

I praise the justice of that light and laughter
Though now it only opens and illuminates
The heart's poor hoard:

Our gossamer ideas,
Our brave and broken stories,
Our small, imperfect
Acts of love:

She leaps again towards the light.

Red – for L

Cochineal, vermillion, madder, rose:
The giant star, the common sun,*
The prohibition and the carnival,
Hyena-feast, god-celebration,
Ibis, orchid, poppy, fire;
The viscous welling which once bore
Dream and desire from shattered brain
To fingertip, to hip, to breast – to us, to him, to her:
All wounds and certain kisses.

Delirious wine and apple biting back,
Red caves of the little hunter, tongue;
Parrot loud, damask soft
Autumn-inferno, Rose of Love,
How white was tempted; black's
Cinderella dream.

Wine of battlefield, wine of death,
How long will you stain the world
With your homicidal sunsets?
This is your commandment, Red:
                    you must forever break
New raucous worlds between a woman's thighs
Until robots fabricate
Their perfect silent kin.

Trace of kisses, trace of crime,
Memento of first love,
Menstrual celebration, as the red moons hunt
Their lovers' caresses, their children's' eyes;
Is it all so sweet, is it all so simple,
This red torrent, this red song?

* The red giant and the red dwarf, the commonest type of star.

Scarlet, ochre, sienna, crimson
Ruby buried deep and rare,
Earth's compression, love's expression,
This hard quintessence adorning skin,
Outlasting memory, deleting touch,
Erasing kisses

Red enough: and lips so greedy, tender,
So wild and sometimes wise.

Red enough: the blood wasted, the dry wombs,
The orchards without blossom,
As if the jig of chromosomes
Could tell us all our tales.

Red enough this poem,
Grey shadow of my blood.
Red enough, and always,

– Your hair upon your naked shoulders

The Names of Moths

Theirs is the litany of twilight:
Marbled Brown and Kentish Glory,
Lesser Lutestring, Frosted Green,
White Satin and Black Arches,
Sallow Kitten, Angle Shades,
The Tigers, Leopards and the Hawks
– Bee, Oleander, Humming Bird –
Great Brocade and Prominent,
The Ghost Swift and the Emerald,
Cinnabar and China Mark
– though moths also know midday

And all the flagrant glories of the sunlit trees.
Which poem will rest this evening
On your jamb or darkening pane
As you are dreaming, resting, planning
For your distant young; what will shelter drab,
                                        unregarded,
What will irk and flicker at your edge of eye?

Moths, for all their grand mythology
Of darkness, flame and sudden death –
Great warrior stuff – make poor samurai,
Their hara-kiri is a tungsten-toasting and they roast out
In pathetic dervish vertigoes,
Displaying little self-control.

I should chant them out of Havisham hovels,
Sour unopened drawers, the rotting beams
And junk-shop vaults of poetry, sing them
All their true ingenious hues
Not dingy smirched or dull
But splendid expedient tints and shades,

Too good for blowsy butterflies,
This subtle complex camouflage
Those repertoires of lichen, twig and leaf,
Of dapple-sun and bark and shadow,
Those new imaginings of grey

But I fall upon my separate night
Choosing coward peace and tepid calm,
Age and rust and flatulence, these are my riches;
I dodge infernos and try the best
To quell my flutterings with self-restraint and pills,
Yet something glimmers in the wheezing dusk;
I loved you once – these are
The names of moths.

Alicia (at a café by Loch Lomond)

Alicia told me
Where lush wood-rush swags the little cliff
And chattering waters cleave
Pale millennia of stone, and "a little beach
With every pebble just the same."

She told me of
Moody briar-tangled burns,
Of bluebell screes (too late!), whole acres, meadows,
Thick with hyacinth; of wider waters
Where the ancient oaks
Almost embrace across the stream.

I walked germander paths
And thought of you, Alicia,
Sloe-haired, slender, laughing, lithe;
Your eyes I magicked speedwell blue;
It was unequalled June and foxglove towers
With soft exotic bells
Summoned all the season's height.

Beneath the amorous oaks,
By riffle, slide and whorling pool,
In the endless hallucinations of the water's skin
I fancied the gestures and expressions
Of an ideal partner, ideal friend,
One who never bored or who could shatter boredom
With a movement or a word.

And yet Alicia, thirty years too young, and I
Too dull to find some master line,
Some stratagem to murder time.

I remember her darkness, sweetness, slender grace,
I call her voice a river, of precious, of far-travelled stones,
I hold that memory, delightful, diamond, adamant
And all her stories of the summer wood;
I remember the hallucinations of the water's skin
For that always which my memory is,
Forever in some deep, refreshing, sunlit vein.

The Dancer of my Dreams

She is the dancer of my dreams
And where she walks
A shadow sears my days,
A glowing shadow
Glanced from Heaven,
Never known till now

And she is all impossibles
Made so full and sweet,
A dancer all her days
– Tender flowing movement,
Fearless spirit in her eyes

Heaven touches earth so lightly,
Glitters, teases, skims
But in all my dreams
That honey-scalding light
Will touch this world again

She is the dancer of my days,
She is all impossibles,
She is now, again, the light of heaven,
– She is the dancer of my dreams.

Ginny Davies

White Duck

The Calder sparkled
In the morning sun
Daffodils nodded their heads
In clumps along the bank
Wild garlic clad the ground.

A lone white duck
Swam with the flow
She swam and swam
The water carrying her down
Over the rocks below.

Through swirling pools
Her pure white feathers
Shimmered in the light
She reached the loch
Freedom now in sight.

Amongst the Mallards
The only white duck
Ruffled herself without fear
She quacked with contentment
As if to say, "I'm here".

Lonely no more
She wallowed in the ripples
Stared into clear water
Felt the freshness of the air
Happy in the sunshine.

I saw her today
As I stopped awhile
Looking proudly white
Twelve babies at her side and . . .
I think I saw her smile.

Her Baby

Why does she scream when I pat her hair,
Her green eyes half shut, peering?
The light is fading as the sun goes down
Her cot rocking with her sadness.
She senses my hands are hard and stiff,
Tenses as I look down on her crumpled face,
I want to hold her hand, kiss her cheek
But as the shadows fall, I stand motionless.

The nurse looks at me with solemn eyes,
Turns her head away and softly sighs.
Like ice on new green grass
Her mother's tears freeze in drops, and dry
As she laughs and tosses her hair,
"Let's go !"

Lost and Found

So this is where you lie
Amidst the holly and the yew.
Like ice on new green grass
My tears freeze in drops
As I try to imagine holding your hand.
But as the shadows fall
I stand motionless,
Leaves fluttering down to land.
In the distance I think I see your face
But my eyes are peering into darkness,
My mind so tired of constant hoping,
You no longer thinking of me . . . thinking of you.

I never knew you.
Did you ever wear an apron,
Or was it pearls or garish earrings,
Or low-cut shiny satin blouses?
I heard you always liked to dance,
"A good time girl" was what they said.
If only I could ask you why,
Why I was abandoned without a sigh,
A foundling babe just ten weeks old,
A lamb discarded from the fold?
Did you not feel sadness and regret?
Did you never want to hold me?
Did you never think of me,
As I now always think of you?
I'm sorry that our paths have never met, but
You did give me something I'll not forget –
Soft with the comfort I never got from you,
I still have my orange bear.

Breaking

Clear lapping waves run out on rippled sand
That distant feeling all is lost and gone
And she is left there standing all alone
With tern and seagulls flying in to land.
The sea the rocks the shore have left a band
Where bits of wood and old tin cans were thrown
It's lonely now and all the birds have flown
The wind and rain with her now hand in hand.

We used to skip and dance and play around
Catch little crabs and fishes in the pools
Why is that now forgotten and not seen.
I wait to hear a voice, some distant sound
As only I would act as all life's fools
To turn the tide to where it's always been.

Attention Seeking

Nosing cat on my pencil as I write,
Soft paws dabbing at my hand,
Velvet fur shining as the sun streams in.
Purring, with whiskers twitching
At every movement of my pen.
He must know that I'm thinking,
But wants the attention he can't get
While I'm working, writing a poem
About a cat.

Grandfather

The days quicken and lengthen as I wait
But what exactly am I waiting for?
Is it the loves and hopes of eighty years
Eighty years of solitude and unhappiness?
I must have noticed birds in trees
Flowers in bud, rabbits at play,
Are not all these things in nature
Worth the time I've spent living?

You must not wait until the end
To look back and reminisce,
All you think is lost continues still.
You had unhappy thoughts I know
Through anger, fear, pain and grief,
But always returned to look at me.
Youth and inspiration can surely
Not be born out of me,
I would not dare to tell you really
That all you have is all I see.
So do not grieve that I have followed you,
I want you to want what I want too.

Yesterday

I saw you yesterday
You were hanging out the washing
on the line shirts and vests not mine
someone else has taken my place
You no longer watching me . . . watching you.

Lone Fox

Fox are you lonely in the long dark night
In your coat so red and your eyes so bright?
As you glide through the forest and over the hill
You roam all night at your own sweet will.
But what are you seeking I'd like to know
As your feet run fast with your body low.
Perhaps you think that you can't be seen,
No one will ever know where you have been.
But I've been watching and I hope I've guessed
You've done with your hunting and you're home
                                    to your nest.

Sadness

Flower pot with green leaves
White lily sprouts in the light
Withers in the night.

Elegy

This stone is supposed
To give your life
A meaning.
It stands alone
Amongst the laurel
And the yew and I
Know that you were loved
Because it says so.

Davie Dougan

Thelma's Itchy Feet!

First met Thelma, we stood at the bus stop.
Eyes tight shut, and her Walkman blared loud.
I looked down – Jeez – Her body was awesome,
Her wee feet moved about on the ground.

I nudged her – "Is this your bus coming?"
I could see she was right far away.
When her eyes opened wide, they were hazel.
"Are you going in to town, for the day"?

I sat next to her; she kept squirming.
"Would you rather not sit next to me?"
I thought; maybe the lassie was freezing
Or was bursting – and needed to pee?

    "Naw. It's jist the good sounds fae mah Walkman
    Though it's aff, the tune's still in mah heid
    It's wan o' they ones you must dance tae
    If ah didnae move, then ah'd be deid"!

"Do you fancy the dancin' on Friday?
I could meet you from work – We'd have tea!
The dancing goes right on till morning
If you'd like, we could stay out till three!"

"I hope you've no 'Man' to get home to
Or your Mum will not kick up a stink
For I'll see you straight home in a taxi."
Thelma just gave a nod, then a wink.

Well, we went every week to the Palais.
She could move and she sure wasn't shy
As we winched in her close, she's still dancing
With that far-away look in her eye.

We got married – Honeymoon was in Blackpool
   "C'moan Davie! – The Tower – Right away!"
I thought, Good! We will see all the landmarks
   "Naw – The Ballroom – Therr's a rerr baun' the day!"

Well we waltzed – We Jived, even Samba'd
All that day – We did not leave the floor.
I said Thelma – "Are you not a bit tired, dear?"
   "Naw, Davie – We kin dance a bit more!"

Finally got her to bed. She's so gorgeous.
I was knackered, my body was sore.
Still her feet moved in bed. As though dancing.
How the hell did I wake on the floor?

Summertime

By here, it's strong, this country air
There's coos an' sheeps jist everywhere.
Wee lambs urr jumpin', 'ziff they're crazy
Sniffin' – Chewin' every daisy.

Isnae any wind a-sighin'
Can't tell the time fae dandelions.
Ah'm gled that ah don't hiv a coat
Fur bye jings – Noo, it's awfy hoat!

Ah'n noo ah'm feelin' near tae death
Say waarm. Ah cannae get mah breath
Ah'd like a breeze, fae a wee fan
Or somethin' cauld, fae an ice-cream van.

Even You Can Write a Story

Where urr ye' aff tae aw dressed up every Monday morning wi' a tie on?

    I go to the Writer's Group in the Library

Oh – Aye – Whit goes on therr?

    A group of aspiring writers meet and discuss each other's work.

Urr ye' a writer then?

    Everybody has a wee story in them – and we all like to put our wee stories on paper. Something like writing an essay at school!

Ah hated writing essays at school. So ah definitely widnae like it.

    Just think. You're good at telling a story or a joke. Why don't you try writing one of your jokes down? It could be good fun, and you could maybe send it in to one of the papers – Who knows, you might even get a few bob back from them! I like that one about the 'Vampires on the car windscreen'!

Ah couldnae dae that – An' anyhow, whit aboot a' the swear words?

    Just imagine that you were telling the joke to your granny!

But mah granny's deid!

    Well, imagine you're telling it to my granny!

But ah don't know your granny.

Write it to that old woman over there! And don't tell me you don't know that old woman over there! Just write the bloody joke down as though you're telling it to any old woman.

Then what?

If you can do that, then it will show that you are some kind of writer!

Me, a writer – You're definitely jokin'!

Well, maybe you could try your hand at poetry?

Poetry – Huh! – That's just for girls and poofs.

I've heard you recite poetry!

Me – Never!

How about that one about the 'Old Man From Kilbirnie" – And I bet that at school you would recite the one about the 'Old Man From Barlinnie'.

But that isnae poetry!

That is poetry. They call it a Limerick. It's an Irish jocular poem.

Jeez oh! Imagine that! Me, recitin' poetry.

Why don't you give it a wee try? Would you not like to come along with me and see what goes on?

Me?
Yes, you!

But – Me? Get away – Ah couldnae write a story! Ah find great difficulty writin' mah name an' address doon, an' that is far less trouble than puttin' sensible words doon oan a bit o' paper.

It's OK fur you sayin' it's nae bother. But it's me you're expectin' tae dae a' the writin'! Where wid ah start? Whit dae ah write aboot?

Ah'm rotten at spellin', an' mah writin' is atrocious, an' anyway, ah hate fillin' in forms! Me write a story – You must be jokin'!

Just write about the first thing that comes into your head.

Well, that would be bevvie.

What else?

Well, there's bevvie, an' then there would be women.

What else?

There's the horses, the bookies, women an' of course bevvie. Oh. Ah think ah said that already?

What do you not want to write about?

Fur a start. Ah don't want tae write wan oh yer stories.

C'mon. There must be something you don't want to write about!

Well, there's next month's rent. Then there's the wife.

Why don't you just write down what we've been talking about!

But we weren't talkin' aboot anythin' – Jist aboot me no' wantin' tae write a blasted story!

Listen – See this conversation. Well, just supposing I was someone else? Now if you met a deaf person. How would you be able to tell them all about what we've been on about? Now don't say it. Don't tell me that you don't know any deaf people!

Try and write down what you think about me! It doesn't matter what you say as long as you get something down on the paper.

Go on. You'll be amazed at what you can turn out and you might even enjoy it! If you like, you can write down what you'd rather be doing right now.

JEEZ OH! Ah've written two pages.

MAGIC! – YOU'VE WRITTEN A STORY! Just let me read it back to you! Now that's a story!

Am I a writer?

You're damn right – **YOU'RE A BLOODY WRITER!**

Heather Hamilton

Invisible Threads

Invisible threads being spun all around me,
Creating the threads of life's mystic tapestry,
Vibrant, eternal, creative and flowing
Essence of all which can't be unwound.

Choices we're making and chances we're taking,
Feeling our way and hoping it's right.
Stretching out softly, trusting our instincts
Hold on to your hats, are we ready for flight?

Pushing the boundaries of life as we know it
Knowledge and passion coming now into sight.
United Nations, trying to stand in the middle,
Sense now of knowing, that the answer's not fight.

Been distrustful and wasteful, selfish and controlling
To long in the dark without enough light,
Lingering shadows now searching for places,
For Want and Destruction's desires to ignite.

Tug on your thread; try to stop it from flowing
And you'll have to repair it again and again,
There's no one but you can hold yours together
Weaving your web, it's the same for all men.

What would we think of viewing such tapestry?
Worlds within worlds spun with this energy.
Intelligent life, well, what is that anyway?
Through our vain eyes would we think it's the enemy
And fear begin once again?

So I leave with a thought that we ought to get spinning
For our part in the tapestry, I would love to be shining
With the colours of love, its threads intertwining
In rivers of life, our own we're designing
With free choice, the key for all wo/ men.

Feeling Their Presence

Sitting one day, trying to distract myself from the chronic
pain in my back, I decided to go into the pain, tension and
negative thoughts I have when pain grips me. I thought I
would try to change how I felt about it and write thoughts
down. This is what came:

In sweet silence I sit, aware of the presence
of their soft gossamer essence, caressing me
with their delicate luminescent flutterings.

It's in unexpected moments that they ache
to stretch out from within, their faint rustlings
reminding me of my eternal existence.
What tales they could speak of: matters, choices
And the conscious awakening to other realms.

Shh, don't tell, it's not for the fainthearted.
Fear might drag them down, down.

I sit in this quiet space, aware of their presence.
It is enough to know their unfolding around me.
Embracing and whispering, as above so below.
Let wisdom have its place from deep rebellion into clarity.
Truly now I ask, let my wings unfold so that I might soar.

That Strange Alien Woman

An alien's what you'd call me
Brought from somewhere deep in space.
The task, to spend time on your planet,
Trying to understand your race.

So much I find disturbing
Through the horrors that I see.
What kind of beings are you?
You stop your own from being free.

Your planet's rich beyond compare,
Yet it's destroyed without a care,
To what the consequence will be,
You have eyes, yet cannot see.

And there's this thing you seem to crave.
This money stuff, is this a game?
I understand it has its place,
But not controlling you, the human race.

I see such dark and deep despair
Lack of respect is everywhere,
Forgetting that you've come so far
Your sacred right, Shine Like a Star.

Such diverse beauty in your forests,
That have been burned down to the ground,
Your world's companions slaughtered
For food and clothing that abounds.

Miraculous seas with life forms teeming,
Wiped out, poisoned, you don't care.
Don't realise they're sacred,
With as much right to live here.

The precious life forms that's your children,
Oh, this hurts me so to say
I watch them cry and die in thousands.
Why are they mistreated in this way?

I know it sounds like there's no hope,
This world is doomed, some pointless joke,
But what I've learned here I can see,
Something that lights the core of me.

A chance for beings everywhere
Is what my heart is finding here.
A beauty that's incredibly rare
The Transformation of what you all Fear.

There's been many beings in the past
Chose to help you understand,
Conversing with, while loving you,
Since humankind began.

These beings look like you and me,
Although vibrate higher with eyes that see,
But even that's misunderstood
You're afraid of change, you're scared of truth.

You're so consumed with being right
You miss the point and turn to fight
You blame each other for what's gone wrong
I hear it in your words and songs

And though my planet's been there too
It seems we learn faster than you do.
We work with the force that binds
Us all together, all forms, all kinds.

Free choice has always been your option,
So make 'good will' your intention.
Get together, people power,
Give what's wrong media attention.

Don't leave it up to someone else,
Distribute wealth till no ill health.
Equality and freedom you know
Would be a better seed to sow.

There feels no place where I fit in,
I try but there's this gap within
I try to blend the best I can
But hear the whisper, strange woman.

I wish you only peace of mind.
I'm not the scary type you'll find.
I observe that's all, so have no fear,
And when that's done, I'll disappear.

So deal with your fears and do it fast,
Being stuck in them means you won't last.
Don't regret your choice as time goes by,
When you could be choosing

Transformation
Like your Butterfly.

Pat Thomson

A Summer's Afternoon

Mother is busy through in the front room, the baby asleep in his cot. I tiptoe across the kitchen floor, out of the door and down the stairs. I go under the porches and run down the terrace until I am far enough away to honestly say I never heard anyone shouting on me.

On through the opening at the end of the houses and out on to the High Street, opposite the row of shops. There's a bookmakers and a shop that lends and sells books, it's called Freddie Jacks. I think the word 'book' attracts me. Further along the street is Miss Wilson's. She sells paraffin and nails and all sorts of things so dear to a man's heart.

On along the street past the Corner Bar, across Factory Street and up the foot of the Johnshill, passing the old churchyard and into the East End. A short way along this road a dirt path [Skippers Path] runs down to the Gates Road. From there it is only a short walk to the West Gates. About halfway between them and the smallholdings I come to a gate. Going through this and across the field, keeping watch for the bull, I come to a stile at the edge of the wood. Climbing over the stile I enter what I call Bluebell Woods. It's lovely and cool among the trees after the heat of the sun. After splashing my face with cold water from the burn and drying it on the hem of my dress, I make my way up through the trees looking for a spot of soft grass where I can stretch out in the warm sunshine. How pleasant it is lying there in the sun, eyes half shut, listening to the distant drone of an aeroplane.

Somewhere near my ear the buzz of a bee collecting pollen and the hum of the insects. Through my half opened eyes I see a deep blue summer sky and the green of the tree tops. A magpie starts flyting somewhere in the woods and the peace of the slumbering afternoon is broken.

I decide it's time to move on but where to go. I think on it for a wee while and decide to go to my granny's. I retrace my steps back to the High Street but carry on past the shops, going along as far as Baird's the grocers on the corner of Craw Road. The wee school is on the opposite corner but is closed for the holidays, so there is no sign of life. I turn up the Craw Road, along the side of Willie Glen's field where they have started building prefabs to house the men returning from the war and their families.

To get to Braehead I go up a track at the side of the field. You have to be careful as there is a burn running down the middle of it. At the top is a gate that opens so you can get out into Braehead. The road consists of council houses built before the war, a cottage and two large houses.

"Any tea in the pot?" I ask as I go into Granny's, "I'm

parched."

The tea is just how I like it, half tar, half water with plenty of milk and sugar.

"Would you like some chocolate?" asks my gran.

"Yes, please," is my reply.

I get handed a full cake of chocolate. This is a great treat with sweets still being on ration.

"You're not going to eat all that chocolate now?" asks Granny.

"Why not, if I take it home I'll have to share it and anyway it'll melt in this heat," I say, "So I may as well eat it". Greedy devil that I am I scoff the lot.

Having been fed and watered I decide it's time to head for home. I go along Braehead and into Calder Street, turning down towards the Cross. On the way I stop to have a look at the forthcoming attractions advertised outside the picture house, otherwise known a Johnny's. I wander on down to the Cross and look along the High Street, wishing I had managed to cadge three pence off one of my aunts for an ice cream from Dom's. I cross over into Church Street looking in John Black's corner window, past Nettie Murray's hairdressers, John Chapman the butcher's and Willie Storrie the barber's. Then comes the police station before Harvey Square. There's the four twenty nine to

Ardrossan leaving the station. Almost home, what a lovely afternoon.

If only it was as easy to turn the clock back for an hour or two to relive days like these instead of drawing on them from memory.

Thoughts

Sitting at the window looking out, as darkness falls, at the chimney pots, the loch and the hills on the other side of the valley, the tops gleaming in the last light of the day. Something makes you think of the people who lived and died in these houses over the years. Were they happy or sad? Did they have a comfortable home? Were they employed in the mills or the furniture works? What did they do in their spare time?

In the late twenties a family of incomers arrived in the village. To provide a living they bought a coal merchant's business. Originally they lived in Calder Street in a house that had stables behind for the horses. The father and eldest son took care of the business, bagging and delivering coal, loading carts and most importantly looking after the horses. I remember being told stories about them.

Each horse had a very distinctive nature and, you could say, was named accordingly. What do you think?

Jet was a black cob who took his time about everything and couldn't be rushed. Every so often he decided to have a holiday; he just lay down in the shafts and refused to work. All they could do was take him back to the stables where he spent the rest of the day, quite happy to return to work the next day. Another horse called Patience would take herself home to the stable whenever the works' hooter went. So, take a bag of coal off the cart and go up a close to put it in the customer's bunker, the 12 o'clock horn goes, no horse and cart! After the 1 o'clock went she would go back to work till 5 o'clock sounded, then off back to the stable for her supper. She would then go back to work and if necessary work until the next morning, when the hooter sounded again. The last and only horse I remember was a Clydesdale called Captain, who a fortnight after he retired tried to jump a fence and broke his leg, and had to be put to sleep. So ended the career of a gentle giant.

Horses were a big part of village life. What is now known as Barr Loch was drained in summer months. The dried grass was cut and used for bedding the beasts. During the Second World War the machinery used for this fell into disrepair. After the war there was no need for the straw, and since the cost of repairing the pump was high, the meadow was allowed to flood.

In the late thirties the family moved to Braehead, into one of the new council houses. The father who was a great "doo" man had a new loft built at the new house. During summer, you would find him there on a Saturday afternoon, waiting on the birds coming in so he could ring them. He would sit on a wooden bench in front of the loft, puffing on a cigarette, until a bird landed on the roof. If it wasn't going in or it took off again he was up with his wee tin of peas, rattling it enticingly to coax the bird into the loft. When it eventually came in the ring was taken from its leg and put in a box which recorded the time. If the pigeon landed early enough and he won, he was as happy as a sandboy but if it didn't he would threaten to wring its neck.

As lorries were taking over from horses it was decided to get one. The son taught himself to drive and to his dying day never sat a driving test. One of his early mishaps was hitting the Village Hall gate post when he was reversing in. The gate post, made of red sandstone and relatively soft, was left a bit shoogly. This gate does not exist any more.

The pace of life must have been much slower than today, when people had time to listen to the peace and quiet. Few cars, no lawn mowers or strimmers to disturb the peace. Does your lawn need cutting? Shove a goat or sheep in for a couple of hours. Not many people then would have had a lawn, perhaps a drying green where they could sit for a few minutes at the end of the day. Most gardens would be used to grow edible plants that could be used to supplement the family budget.

When I was a girl the garden at the stables still existed and, in season, all the soft fruit it was possible to grow were there as well as apple and pear trees. Many a warm summer afternoon I've spent filling my face with this bounty from nature.

Deborah Winters

Hallowe'en

Round the neighbours' doors they straggle,
Village children in a gaggle,
Snow White and Red Riding Hood,
Pocahontas looking good,
David Beckham, Superman
And in behind comes Wee Batman.

Super outfits bought in Tesco,
Party dresses worn al fresco.
"Who can this be?" we all wonder.
"It's me, it's me!" Wee Batman blunders.
"Surely not, what a surprise,
That's a really great disguise!"

They sing their songs and tell their jokes,
Accept their apples and nuts in pokes,
Excitedly go on their way
Another neighbour to waylay.
I watch them wistfully and sigh
And think of Hallowe'ens gone by.

Times when folk were more contented,
Supermarkets weren't invented.
Money was in short supply,
None to spare, you just 'got by'.
No dress-up outfits from the shops,
You just made do with old cast-offs.

Your Mum's old dress, a bit of lace,
Soot from the lum to black your face,
Father's jacket, cap and pants,
A fancy necklace of your aunt's.
Round the village sing your song,
Fun and laughter all night long.

Nowadays fun's electronic,
Digital or supersonic.
Cyberspace is where they play.
"Times have changed," you hear folk say.
But yet they seem still to be keen
To go out on Galloshens at Hallowe'en.

The Uphill Path

A narrow winding uphill road
Draws me onward,
After the slow plodding, plodding
With wet mud-caked boots
Through the dark slimy pit bottom
Of the valley.

Finger-scrabbling, toe-clinging pull, pull
Up the slippery slopes,
Gaining ground thrice lost,
Only to be sucked back
By the fast downward spiral
Of Panic and Defeat.

How will I reach a place
Where I can see the sun,
Bask in her warm kindness,
Thaw ice-bound limbs,
Pamper the ravaged spirit?
Return to the land of Before?

Rest here awhile?
Imprisoned
In the black bog-bottom of Despair?
Wait here amongst the tombs
For a voice to say,
"Take my hand, I will release you"?

Panic seizes my throat,
Choking me with his terrors.
A warning voice reaches me,
"No one passes this way, none,
This is the country of Alone.
No sun has warmed this place.
Rest here at your peril."

So I rise again,
Reach, reach out, grasp the straw
Of my own faint spirit,
The pale wisp of hope
In this my dark dungeon of weakness.

Highland Haiku

Loud skirl of bagpipes
Stick thin legs and kilts flying
Medalbright eyes glint.

Iona's Invitation to Rothesay Highland Games

"You have to come this Saturday
It's Rothesay Highland Games.
We've got our outfits ready.
Chloe's and mine are the same.

We've entered for the Highland Fling,
High Cuts and Pas de Bas,
We're practicing the Sword Dance
But the Seann Triobhas* is too hard.

I'm going to get a medal
And march behind the band,
Chloe will get a medal too,
We'll be marching hand in hand.

We'll listen for the music
The piper plays so loud,
Point our toes and dance so lightly
And make Miss Anne feel proud.

We'll hold up our bright medals
As we follow the massed pipe bands,
Chloe and I will be happy
When we're marching hand in hand."

*Seann Triobhas pronounced shawn trews.

Quina

Yellow lichen grows on the stones
Of the house that looks over the loch.
Flag iris cluster around the old well
By brecks where wild lupins grow.

Docken and nettles usurp the place
Where rhubarb and blackcurrants grew
But honeysuckle still covers the wall,
Young Ellen planted it there.

Willie had built a fine house for her
When first she had come as his bride.
He quarried the stone and built the stout walls
To shelter their bairns from the storm.

Good land, well tended, provided
Enough for their needs and to spare,
Blue peats from the hill in the inby fire,
Box beds, full girnal, straw-backed chair.

Up with the dawn you would hear them,
A low murmur solemn and clear
Praising their Maker and reading the Word
That kept them in surety there.

The old house still stands on the brae,
The welcome it once had, no more.
The bairns are grown old and the old folks gone
And nobody seems to care.

Waves of scent waft o'er the stone wall,
As sweet as the memory it stirs
Of the warmth and the kindness that shone from the face
Of the ones who made this a home.

Eyrland

Here on the shore where my forefathers stood
I feel the timeless scene
Open before me of sea, rock and sand,
Wide bays and pastures green.

Flower strewn meadows and low rolling hills
Deep fringed by salt sea foam,
Beckoning Rognvald of Mor and his men
To make this land their home.

Long, long ago they came, west over sea,
Drawn by the lure of the isles
Told of in tales by adventurers brave
Faring the long sea miles.

Glad when at last they saw fair low green islands,
Hastened to make landfall.
Hauled up their craft on the wide sandy bay,
At Eyrland, built their Hall.

Tilled the land, sowed the seed, made a spring Viking.
Plundered all the west coast.
Brought in the harvest, brewed plenty ale,
Wild escapades to toast.

Sons of the isles go a-viking no more.
Gone are the longships of old,
But many's the tale on a Winter's night
Of ventures brave and bold.

Yet still I stand on the shore and look out,
And think of days that are gone,
Feeling the pull that those people of yore,
Felt for their island home.

Biographical Notes

Joyce Allwright lives in sheltered housing. Retired up here from London to be with her daughter and grandchildren. Although retired, plenty to do in the village. Hobbies: walking, swimming and travel, besides writing.

Clive Briggs is a retired engineering manager well qualified technically who took up creative writing for his own amusement. He finds it socially interesting and it provides the opportunity to express his views and maintain a voice in the community.

Moira Bromley-Wiggins loves living in Lochwinnoch. During 15 years employment in theatre she has had over 50 addresses and worked in 3 separate countries. One of these was Kenya, an experience that figures most often in her writing. Her passion though is dancing, particularly Ceilidh but she has recently taken up classes in Argentinean tango and ballroom, and is finding them both a challenge and an alternative inspiration for writing.

James F. Carnduff has written poems, short stories, including an autobiographical story called *The Joys of National Service in the R.A.F, 1949-1951*. At present he is writing a sci-fi story and is working on his third children's story. Has been a member of the Lochwinnoch Writers' Group since its inception.

Geoff Cooper has lived in Lochwinnoch for six years. Lucky enough to live right by the loch. Has ancestors (Barrs) from the area. Won the Scottish International Poetry Competition in 1994 (possibly a clerical error!).

Ginny Davies was born in London but has lived most of her life in Scotland. She was a professional clarinettist and joined the Royal Scottish National Orchestra after graduating from the Royal College of Music in London. She has played in orchestras throughout Britain, Europe and North America and was a founder member of Scotland's renowned Paragon Ensemble.

Since retiring she has begun writing poetry and joined the Lochwinnoch Writers after completing an OU poetry course. Her other interests include gardening, reading, yoga, theatre and she is an animal lover.

Davie Dougan: After doing his National Service in the RAF as an engine fitter, he wasted the rest of his life in various labouring and machine operator type jobs. On retiring, he has spent most of his spare time attempting to gain the qualifications he never got at school. This wasn't too rewarding! During this period it was discovered that he was epileptic. To try and keep myself occupied he then tried to learn various hobbies.

He did not do too bad at Calligraphy and dabbled in watercolour painting until his hands got too shaky to do straight lines. Along the way he picked up some worthwhile attributes, not least, the knack of writing what he likes to call poetry, which would give the reader a chuckle. This little 'talent' gets an outlet with the Writers' Group, which he's been enjoying for more than three years.

Heather Hamilton moved to Lochwinnoch with her son three years ago and thought she would try writing when she saw the class advertised.

Gerry Stewart is a writer, creative writing tutor and freelance editor. Her first solo book of poetry will be published by Flambard Press in 2007. She is currently on maternity leave from the Lochwinnoch Writers, but hopes to join them again soon.

Pat Thomson is a local resident who joined the writers' club at the end of last year. She would recommend anyone who would like to write to come along and see what we do.

Deborah Winters is from Kilmacolm where she was postmistress, now retired. She enjoys painting, writing, gardening, IT projects, grandchildren and reading. She has Orkney connections and explores her love of the Northern Isles in writing and painting.